EXPLORING THE SOLAR SYSTEM

MOON

GILES SPARROW

Heinemann Library
Chicago, Illinois

MOON

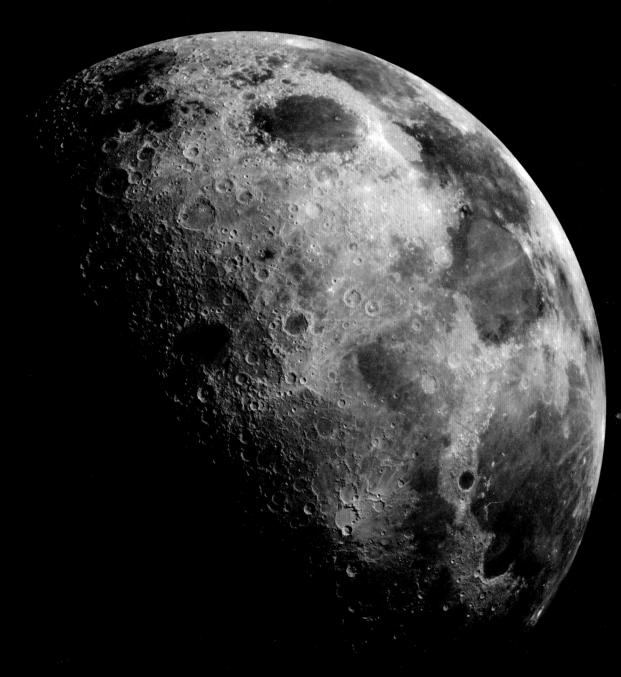

Published by Heinemann Library,
an imprint of Reed Educational & Professional Publishing,
100 N. LaSalle, Suite 300, Chicago, IL 60602
Customer Service 888-454-2279
Visit our website at www.heinemannlibrary.com

Produced by Brown Partworks
Project Editor: Ben Morgan
Deputy Editor: Sally McFall
Managing Editor: Anne O'Daly
Designer: Michael LeBihan
Illustrator: Mark Walker
Picture Researcher: Helen Simm
Consultant: Peter Bond

© 2002 Brown Partworks Limited

Printed in Singapore

ISBN 1-57572-390-5 (hardback)   ISBN 1-58810-963-1 (paperback)
06 05 04 03 02 01   06 05 04 03 02 01
10 9 8 7 6 5 4 3 2 1   10 9 8 7 6 5 4 3 2 1

Library of Congress Cataloging-in-Publication Data

Sparrow, Giles.
  Moon / Giles Sparrow.
      p. cm. -- (Exploring the solar system)
  Includes bibliographical references and index.
    1. Moon--Juvenile literature. [1. Moon.] I. Title.
    QB582 .S68 2001
    523.3--dc21
                                    00-010440

BELOW: *The planets of the solar system, shown in order from the Sun:
Mercury, Venus, Earth, Mars, Jupiter, Saturn, Uranus, Neptune, Pluto.*

CONTENTS

*Some words are shown in bold, like this.
You can find out what they mean by looking in the glossary.*

The Moon is our nearest neighbor in space, situated on Earth's cosmic doorstep at a mere 238,750 miles (384,400 kilometers) away on average. The Moon is our planet's natural **satellite,** held in **orbit** around Earth by the force of **gravity.** It goes around the Earth once every 27.3 days in an orbit shaped like an **ellipse.** At its closest approach the Moon is just 221,462 miles (356,410 kilometers) away from Earth, while at its most distant it is 252,698 miles (406,679 kilometers) away.

Within the solar system, Earth and Moon orbit the Sun at an average distance of 93 million miles (150 million kilometers) once every 365.25 days. The Earth is the third planet from the Sun, and the largest of the four inner **terrestrial** planets. In order from the Sun, these are Mercury, Venus, Earth, and Mars. Beyond Mars lies the **asteroid belt,** an area of rocky **debris** left over from the formation of the solar system, and beyond that is the home of the giant planets—Jupiter, Saturn, Uranus, and Neptune. The most distant planet is small, icy Pluto, just one member of an outer belt of icy objects called the Kuiper Belt.

Getting to the Moon

The Moon is much closer to Earth than the nearest planets, yet it is still a great distance away. The time it takes to get there depends on how you travel.

Distance from Earth to the Moon
Closest   **221,462 miles**
                       (356,410 km)
Furthest   **252,698 miles**
                       (406,679 km)

By car at 70 miles per hour
(113 km per hour)
Closest   **132 days**
Furthest   **150 days**

By rocket at 7 miles per second
(11 km per second)
Closest   **9 hours**
Furthest   **10 hours**

Time for radio signals to reach the Moon (at the speed of light)
Closest   **1.19 seconds**
Furthest   **1.36 seconds**

Distance from Earth

This diagram shows the size of Earth and the Moon and the distance between them exactly

 Earth

Imagine you're going on a **mission** to the Moon. The Moon is very near on the scale of the solar system, but your journey will still take a long time. A powerful rocket could cross the distance from Earth to the Moon in less than ten hours, but your journey will take much longer— three whole days, in fact. This is because you can't travel in a straight line to the Moon. Instead, you have to travel along a figure-of-eight path that will put you into orbit around the Moon. Also, you have to allow time for your spacecraft to speed up and then slow down.

Your spacecraft is just the top part of a huge rocket. Most of the rocket is taken up by the fuel tanks needed to launch your craft into space and escape the pull of Earth's gravity. Once the fuel is used up, the bottom part of the rocket will separate and drop back to Earth. When you reach the halfway point to the Moon, your spacecraft will turn around and travel backward. Small rockets on the craft will then begin firing to slow you down.

This artist's impression shows the planets of the inner solar system: Mercury, Venus, Earth, and Mars. You can also see the asteroid belt and the Moon as it orbits Earth.

Size compared to Earth

*Moon's **diameter**: 2,159 miles (3,475 km)*

Earth's diameter: 7,926 miles (12,756 km)

Moon

200,000 miles (321,860 km)

300,000 miles (482,790 km)

First View

From Earth the Moon is a beautiful sight. It is 400 times smaller than the Sun, but it is also 400 times closer to Earth, so from Earth the Moon and Sun look the same size. Unlike the Sun, the Moon shines only by reflecting sunlight. Although it looks bright in the night sky, its surface is actually very dark and reflects back only a small amount of the light falling onto it.

Because the Moon moves around Earth, we see it lit from different angles, and this causes lunar **phases.** When the Moon lies between Earth and the Sun, the Sun shines on its far side and we cannot see it. This is called a new moon. A week later, the Moon has moved so that half the visible side is sunlit—this is the first quarter. By the next week, the Moon is opposite the Sun and its Earth-facing side is flooded with sunlight—a full moon. The Moon takes 27.3 days to **orbit** Earth, but a full cycle of lunar phases takes 29.5 days because Earth is moving around the Sun at the same time.

You can see patterns on the Moon's surface easily from Earth, even without binoculars. These light and dark patches never change because the Moon keeps the same side facing us all the time. The side we can't see is called the far side.

LEFT: *A huge Saturn V rocket takes off on a **mission** to the Moon. These rockets were as tall as a 32-story building and used up 13 ton of fuel per second as they took off.*

ABOVE: *The Moon's phases are shown here in order from top to bottom. When the Moon is growing in size it is said to be* **waxing.** *As it shrinks back to a new moon, it is **waning.***

Getting Closer

Your journey to the Moon starts spectacularly. You blast off from Earth in a spacecraft atop a huge rocket that will lift you away from the pull of Earth's **gravity.** As the rocket pushes its way up and out of the **atmosphere,** the roar of its engine is deafening. The rocket's acceleration increases your weight to many times its usual value, pushing you down into your seat. It takes just a few minutes to get into space. Then, suddenly, the engine stops firing and you become weightless. The spacecraft is now completely silent, and everything inside it floats in midair.

Crossing the gap between Earth and the Moon takes three days. From space the view of the Moon's surface is crystal clear, and the dividing line between the daytime and nighttime sides is razor sharp. When you shield your eyes from the glare of the daylit side, you notice that the dark side is glowing faintly. This is called Earthshine. The Moon is flooded with light reflected off Earth in just the same way as night on Earth is lit by moonlight.

As you get closer to the Moon, you begin to see surface details with the naked eye. There seem to be two main types of surface on the Moon—bright areas covered with circular **impact craters** of all sizes, and darker, flat plains with far fewer craters.

BELOW: *This photograph of the Moon was taken by the* Galileo *spacecraft. It shows some of the features we can see from Earth, such as craters and dark, flat areas called lunar seas.*

9

The Surface of the Moon

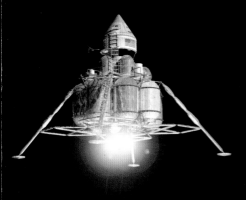

ABOVE: *This artist's impression shows a lunar lander—a small spacecraft used to touch down on the Moon's surface. The lander uses a rocket engine to slow its descent.*

Leaving your main spacecraft in **orbit,** you board a **lander** to visit the Moon's surface. You steer toward an area of rolling hills, carefully avoiding crater edges or steep slopes that might be dangerous to land on. There is no turbulence as you approach because the Moon has no air to blow your craft about. A few hundred yards above the surface, the lander's rockets fire to slow your fall. Their blast raises a dust storm below—you hope that the ground will be firm enough to take your weight! The engines turn off, and you gently drop the last few inches, landing in another puff of dust. The lander rocks slightly before steadying. You now become aware of the Moon's weak **gravity,** which is just a sixth of that on Earth. You can't wait to get outside and bound around on the surface, at a sixth of your Earth weight.

*This amazing lunar landscape greeted the astronauts of the Apollo 17 **mission** to the moon in 1972. The astronauts used a car called the Lunar Roving Vehicle to explore.*

As you step outside in your spacesuit, the lunar soil crumbles beneath your boots. You reach down and pick some up—it seems to be a mixture of ground-up rocks of all sizes. Looking around, you feel your eyes gradually adjust to the brightness, and you see that the landscape is made up of varying shades of gray, with a hint of rusty red. You've landed near a small **impact crater,** and you bound over to its edge in giant strides. Impact craters form when **comets, asteroids,** or **meteorites** crash into planets or moons. This one is bowl-shaped, with steep sides and a sharp rim. On Earth craters are soon worn away by wind and rain, but on the Moon they stay unchanged for millions of years.

You climb a hill for a view across the land. The horizon looks very odd—it seems too close and has an obvious curve. Because the Moon is much smaller than Earth, its round shape is more noticeable. The Sun is blazing down, but when you turn your back on it you can see stars. You can also see a half-Earth, looking tiny in the vast darkness of space.

BELOW: *You would die instantly if you stood on the Moon without a spacesuit. The suit provides air and warmth and contains a two-way radio for speaking to other astronauts. This picture shows astronaut Buzz Aldrin during the Apollo 11 mission of 1969.*

The Lunar Seas

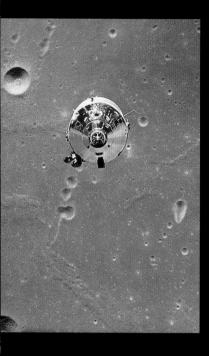

You return in the **lander** to your spacecraft and fly a few hundred feet above the Moon's surface, looking down at the landscape. A great plain of bare rock rolls by below like a vast ocean—in fact, it's called the Sea of Tranquility. The first people to make maps of the Moon thought these flat plains looked like oceans. This one is a historic landmark: the first moon landing took place here in 1969.

The lunar seas are called **maria** in Latin (pronounced *mar*-ee-ah), and the cratered areas between them are called highlands, or **terrae** (*ter*ree). As you fly near the edge of the sea you notice that it appears to have flowed into the highlands! The bottoms of some of the valleys and craters in the highlands are filled with the same flat rock that forms the seas.

Sea of Rains

Ocean of Storms

ABOVE: *An Apollo spacecraft flies over the Sea of Fertility during the* Apollo 11 *mission to the Moon in 1969. This picture was taken from a lander (the Lunar Module).*

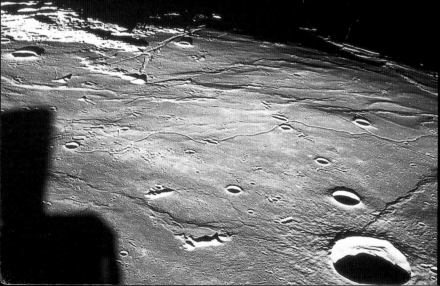

LEFT: *This photograph of the Sea of Tranquility was taken by* Apollo 11 *astronauts. The very long channels running across the top of the photograph are called rilles. At the bottom right is the Maskelyne Crater.*

LEFT: This photograph of the Moon shows the main seas, or maria smooth, dark areas formed by lava filling up craters on the surface

Sea of Serenity

Sea of Crises

Sea of Tranquility

This pattern is repeated all over the Moon's surface and shows that the maria formed after the highlands. In so cases the maria even wiped out parts of the highlands.

You're approaching the **terminator** now—the line that divides night from day on the Moon. As the Sinks in the sky behind you, the shadows it casts grow longer, revealing more detail. You dip close preparation for a landing on the sea, and you notice that the surface isn't entirely flat. In some places it's wrinkled or cracked. A strange, snakel valley called a rille stretches across it.

After landing, you collect and analyze some rock samples. The lunar seas are made of **basalt,** an ir rich **mineral** that is also common on Earth. Basalt forms when molten rock, such as **lava,** cools down and solidifies—so the lunar seas must have formed from gigantic floods of lava. The Moon's basalt is very similar to Earth's basalt, apart from the fact that it doesn't contain any water.

How the maria formed

The lunar seas, or maria, formed from huge floods of lava. The lava erupted from the Moon's interior millions of years ago and swept across the surface, as shown in the illustrations below. Because maria have few craters on their surfaces, they must have formed after the major cratering that peppered the Moon's surface. In fact, some of the biggest craters, called **basins,** are filled in with maria. The wrinkles are a result of the maria distorting as they pushed down on the **crust** below. The rilles are channels along which lava once flowed.

Lunar crater before volcanic lava flood

Lava flood forming a new sea

Hills and Hollows

It's time to take a closer look at the lunar highlands. You fly away from the flat plain and over the high ground that rises beyond the "shore." It's hard to make sense of the jumbled landscape below you. **Impact craters** of all sizes stretch as far as the eye can see, and some have bright rays spreading out around them, running across the surrounding ground. Here and there, boulders lie randomly in the middle of the landscape.

The highlands cover most of the Moon's surface and are much brighter than the dark **maria,** making you wonder if the two areas are made of different types of rocks. You land again, this time in the shadow of a boulder the size of a house, and take some more rock samples. You were right: these rocks are much less **dense** and contain far less iron than rocks from the maria. Geologists call the highland rocks plagioclase feldspar. The rocks are rich in silica—a mineral found in sand on Earth—and rich in light **elements,** such as aluminum and calcium. These light materials floated to the surface when the Moon was younger and its outer layers were molten. Heavier materials such as iron sank below the **crust** and erupted later to form the maria.

BELOW: *An **astronaut** holds a sample of moondust during the Apollo 12 **mission**—the second landing on the Moon. You can see the dust nearly filling the container. You can also see the photographer reflected in the astronaut's visor.*

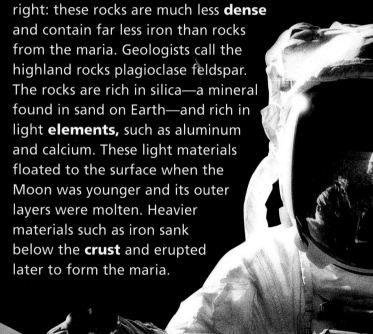

14

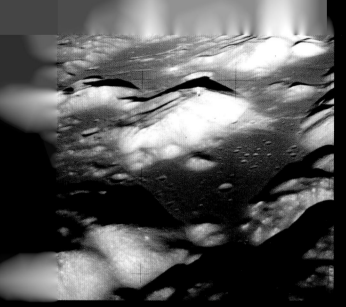

The highlands show signs of heavy cratering. The boulder you're standing next to, and the bright rays your ship flew across, make up an **ejecta blanket**—material flung out from an **impact crater** when a **meteorite** or other object hit the Moon.

Earth's **atmosphere** protects us from meteorite collisions. Most pieces of space **debris** burn up as they hit the atmosphere, turning into shooting stars. Only very large meteorites—or even bigger objects like **comets** and **asteroids**—make it to the ground and produce craters. Over time, the effects of rain, rivers, ice, and wind, and the movement of Earth's crust wipe out all our craters. But on the Moon there is no atmosphere or weather, so the surface has kept a perfect record of even the tiniest impacts over billions of years.

ABOVE: *This photograph shows the highland landing site of the* Apollo 17 *mission—the last crewed trip to the Moon. The valleys between the hills have filled with lava from the nearby Sea of Serenity.*

Moondust

The entire surface of the Moon is covered in a layer of crushed and powdered rocks called the **regolith***. This is the result of millions of years of bombardment from space by tiny* **micrometeorites***, which have gradually worn the surface down to a powder. Larger impacts melted areas of the regolith, and when they solidified again,* **breccias** *formed. These are large rocks formed from smaller fragments that stuck together. Because the Moon has no wind or water to wear down its surface, this astronaut's footprint in the regolith could last for millions of years.*

Craters, Craters Everywhere

Lunar **impact craters** are a vital source of information for astronomers. Because they are well preserved and rarely wiped out, astronomers can tell the age of different parts of the Moon's surface simply by counting the craters.

Cratering has not been steady throughout history, however. When the solar system formed about 4.6 billion years ago, there was much more **debris** floating around in space and bombarding the Moon. The rate of cratering gradually fell, but for some reason it increased again about 3.9 billion years ago in a period called the **late heavy bombardment.** This storm of impacts pulverized the Moon in a relatively short time, creating the jumbled terrain that covers the highlands today. About 3.85 billion years ago, the late heavy bombardment came to an end with several catastrophic collisions. These produced gigantic craters called **basins.** The rate of impacts then fell to a very low level, which has continued until today.

ABOVE: *Astronaut Charles Duke, Jr., stands next to Plum Crater during the Apollo 16 mission. The metal stick is a device used to collect a deep soil sample from near the crater rim.*

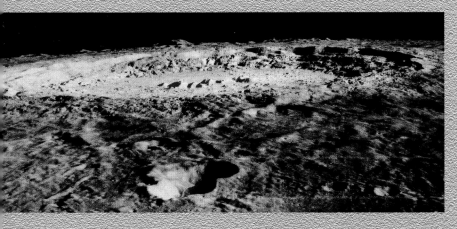

LEFT: *Copernicus Crater is 58 miles (93 kilometers) wide and a billion years old, which makes it one of the Moon's youngest craters. In this photograph you can see hills in the center of the crater. These formed when the ground bounced back after impact.*

16

RIGHT: *Copernicus Crater appears on the horizon in this photograph from the Apollo 17 spacecraft. The flat land around the crater is the Sea of Rains.*

Most of the volcanic eruptions that formed the **maria** happened shortly after the late heavy bombardment, between 3.8 and 3.1 billion years ago. But some maria must be younger because they have very few craters, and in places they overlap freshly made impact craters. As a result, astronomers think volcanic eruptions may have happened on the Moon as recently as a billion years ago.

Craters give astronomers an indirect way of seeing the Moon's interior. When large craters form, material from deep underground gets flung across the Moon's surface. Rocks from close to the surface are flung furthest, while deeper material ends up scattered near the crater rim.

Deep impact

*Impact craters like Schmidt Crater (left) form when a **meteorite**, **comet**, or **asteroid** smashes into the surface of the Moon at tremendous speed. The collision is so violent that the object explodes and vaporizes, leaving almost no trace of it behind. The ground below the impact gets squashed very suddenly and melts, but then it rebounds with great force. The rebound flings debris across the landscape in an **ejecta blanket**, sometimes in rays that stretch hundreds of miles. Craters made by objects more than a few miles wide often have hills in the middle where the ground bounced back.*

17

The Far Side

You've only seen the near side of the Moon so far, so you decide to take a look at the far side. As you steer your ship around the Moon, you see Earth sinking toward the lunar horizon behind you and setting. A strange new landscape opens up ahead.

The far side of the Moon is an alien world compared to the highlands and seas of the near side. It is battered all over with deep craters, and there are almost no **maria.** Your ship's instruments show that the ground varies in height much more on this side of the Moon. On the near side the surface height varies by about 3 miles (5 kilometers) from the bottom of the deepest craters to the tops of the tallest hills. But on the far side the surface height varies by up to 10 miles (16 kilometers). This range of heights is like going from the bottom of Earth's deepest ocean trench to the top of Mount Everest.

Near the south **pole** you see a colossal crater surrounded by mountainous walls. This is the South Pole-Aitken Basin—the biggest **impact crater** known to science, and more than 1,550 miles (2,500 kilometers) across. Unlike the craters on the near side, it was never filled by **lava** to form a sea. Its bottom is scattered with other huge craters, some of which are so deep that their bases never see the light of day.

ABOVE: *The far side of the Moon has more craters than the near side because few maria formed here. Perhaps the far side's thicker crust prevented lava from breaking out easily.*

LEFT: *This photograph was taken on the Moon's far side during the Apollo 11 mission. It shows the International Astronomical Union No. 308 crater (top center), which is 50 miles (80 kilometers) wide, with terraced walls.*

What's Inside the Moon?

Back on the near side of the Moon, it's time to get on with your **mission.** One important task is to set up some **seismometers.** These instruments can measure the **moonquakes** that regularly shake the lunar surface, telling you a little about the inside of the Moon.

Some moonquakes are caused by the pull of Earth's **gravity,** but others are **shockwaves** from the steady stream of **micrometeorites** that hit the Moon. As the shockwaves pass through the different layers inside the Moon, they speed up or slow down. Astronomers can monitor these shockwaves and use them to figure out maps of the Moon's interior.

The **regolith** of pulverized lunar rocks you're standing on extends down for several miles. Beneath this lies a deeper layer of fractured rocks, which broke apart in the **late heavy bombardment** but were forced back together by the Moon's **gravity.** Then there's a solid **crust** reaching down to an average depth of 44 miles (71 kilometers).

Below the Moon's crust lies a **mantle** of once-molten but now solid rock. This may extend all the way through the Moon, occupying 90 percent of the interior, but there could be a small iron **core** at the center. The Moon has a low **density,** which suggests that such a core could not be large. Because the Moon does not have the **magnetic field** that a molten iron core would generate, any core must also be solid.

BELOW: *This diagram shows (from the outside in): the lunar regolith, crust, mantle, and core. The thickness of the crust varies from tens of miles to more than 60 miles (100 kilometers) deep. It is thinnest under the maria and thickest under the highlands of the far side.*

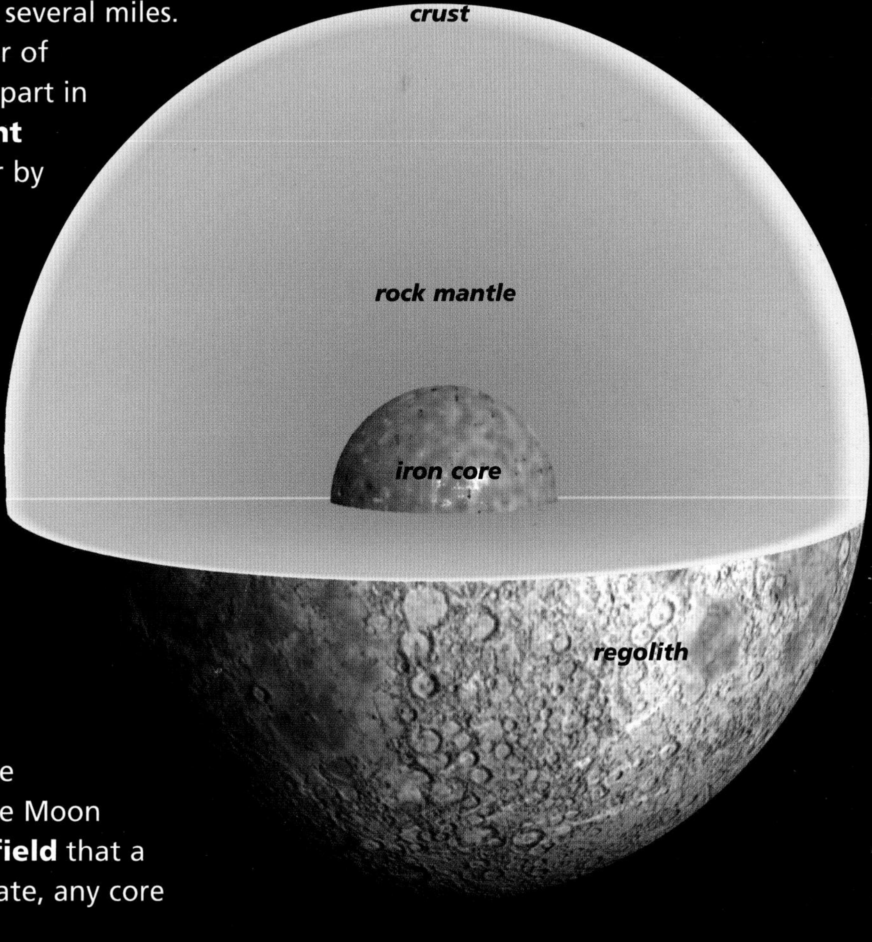

crust

rock mantle

iron core

regolith

How the Moon Formed

All the samples you've collected show that the Moon contains the same **minerals** that are found on Earth, and this suggests that the Moon and Earth formed together. But there's something odd: the minerals are in completely different proportions. For instance, the Moon contains a lot of silica, but very little iron. It is also much less **dense** than Earth. So how could our Moon have formed?

BELOW: *Around 4.5 million years ago, Earth may have been hit by another planet. The collision would have thrown a vast cloud of debris into space, much of which would have become trapped in **orbit** by gravity. The debris eventually clumped together to form the Moon, as shown in this artist's impression.*

Astronomers used to have three main theories about the Moon's formation. Some believed that Earth and the Moon formed at the same time, or that the young Earth spun so rapidly that it flung off a chunk of material to form the Moon. Others believed that the Moon formed separately in a different part of the solar system and was later captured by Earth's **gravity.** But there are problems with all these theories—the first two can't explain why the Moon's composition is different from Earth's, and the third can't explain the similarities between them.

Today nearly all astronomers agree on a different theory—that the Moon formed in a collision. At some point in the early history of Earth, long before life had begun, our planet may have collided with another planet about the size of Mars. The enormous explosion vaporized huge amounts of both planets and blasted **debris** into orbit around them. Lighter materials from their **crusts** and **mantles** ended up in orbit, while the iron **cores** of the two planets merged together.

In the aftermath of the collision, Earth gradually healed itself, and the materials left in orbit began to collide and stick together, eventually building up to form the Moon. According to computer simulations of the process, the Moon could have formed in just a few years.

The collision idea is the first theory to explain why the Earth and Moon are so similar and yet so different. It explains the shortage of lunar iron and also the absence of certain minerals and **elements**—these turned to gas in the explosion and boiled away into space. At least for the moment, it's the best theory astronomers have to explain the origin of the Moon.

ABOVE: *This view through a microscope shows a thin slice of lunar rock magnified 20 times. Geologists have discovered that lunar rock is made of the same minerals found in Earth's rocks. The sample was collected during the* Apollo 11 **mission.**

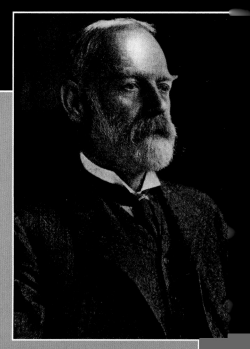

Sir George Darwin (1845–1912)

In the early 20th century most astronomers believed in the theory of the Moon's formation proposed by English astronomer George Darwin. George was the son of the famous naturalist Charles Darwin (1809–1882), and was professor of astronomy at Cambridge University, England. In 1884 he published a detailed analysis of how Earth's gravity affects the Moon. Darwin realized that the Moon is slowly getting further from Earth, which means it must once have been much closer. This led him to think that the two worlds had originated as one rapidly spinning object that separated. However, in the 1930s astronomers figured out that the young Earth could not possibly have spun rapidly enough to fling off the Moon.

A Double Planet

Because the Moon is so large and **orbits** quite close to Earth, its **gravity** has a great effect on our planet—and Earth's gravity in turn affects the Moon. Over billions of years the two worlds have become locked together. Some people even consider Earth and the Moon to be a double planet.

The most obvious effect of the Moon on Earth is the tides. The twice-daily rise and fall of the sea is caused by a bulge in Earth's oceans where water has been tugged toward the Moon by gravity. The tidal bulge always remains broadly in line with the Moon, and is balanced by another bulge on the opposite side of Earth. As Earth **rotates,** both bulges sweep around the planet, causing high tides roughly every twelve hours and low tides about six hours after the high tides. The Sun also contributes to the tides. When the Sun lines up with a new or full moon, its gravity adds to the Moon's and causes a bigger bulge, creating particularly high **spring tides.** During the first and third quarters of the Moon, the Sun's gravity tends to pulls in other directions, evening out the effect and creating lower **neap tides.**

Just as the Moon causes tides on Earth, Earth creates "tides" on the Moon. But there are no oceans on the Moon, so Earth's **tidal forces** act instead on the Moon's movement. After the Moon formed, the constant tug of Earth's gravity slowed down its rotation until the Moon had one side permanently facing us. The Moon now makes one full rotation for each orbit around Earth. Earth's gravity may also explain why **maria** formed mostly on the near side of the Moon. The heavy materials in the Moon's molten interior were pulled close to the **crust** by Earth's gravity, making eruptions much more likely on the near

ABOVE AND BELOW: *The Moon and Earth have a strong effect on each other. Earth's strong gravity holds the Moon in orbit around us, while the Moon's gravity causes the Earth's oceans to rise and fall in a cycle we call tides.*

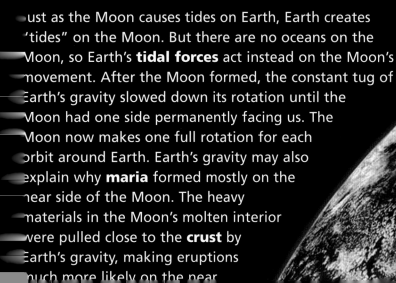

Another effect of tidal forces is that the Moon's orbit is changing. The Moon gets about 1.2 inches (3 centimeters) further from Earth every year, and takes slightly longer to travel around its orbit. At the same time, the pull of the Moon on Earth is slowing our planet's rotation. About 300 million years ago, a day on Earth was only 21 hours long!

The Moon may act as a protector of Earth. Some astronomers think that it soaks up many of the **meteorites** and **asteroids** that get close to Earth, shielding our planet from impacts and so helping to provide a stable environment for life.

A harbor in Polperro in Cornwall, England, shows the difference between the ocean level at low tide (left) and high tide (right).

What causes tides?

The strong pull of the Moon's gravity causes water on the side of Earth closest to the Moon to bulge outward. Water on Earth's opposite side, where the Moon is furthest away and its gravity is weakest, also bulges. These two bulges form the high tides, and the lower areas between form low tides. Because of Earth's rotation, the bulges form slightly ahead of the Moon instead of directly in line with it.

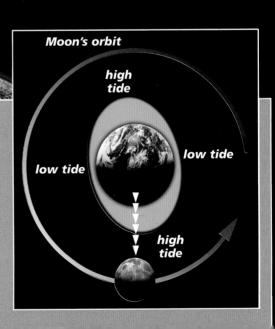

Eclipses

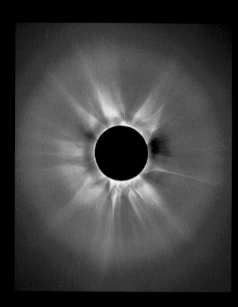

When a new moon passes directly over the Sun's face, it creates one of nature's most spectacular special effects—a total solar **eclipse.** Day turns into night in a matter of seconds, and the air grows suddenly cold. For a few minutes the Sun's beautiful outer **atmosphere,** or corona, is visible. Then, as quickly as it began, the eclipse is over and the Sun reappears.

LEFT: *During a solar eclipse the Moon completely covers the Sun, leaving only the hot gases of the Sun's outer **atmosphere** visible.*

BELOW: *A lunar eclipse happens when Earth's shadow falls on the Moon. Some sunlight is deflected onto the Moon by Earth's atmosphere, which turns the Moon red. In this photograph the brightest edge of the Moon is just emerging from Earth's shadow.*

A solar eclipse happens every one or two years, but you need to be in the right place to see it. When the Moon's small shadow crosses Earth it creates a shadow track thousands of miles long but only a few miles wide. Only the people in this shadow track see the total eclipse. As a result, any particular place on Earth will experience a total solar eclipse just once every few hundred years.

Solar eclipses are dangerous. You should *never* look at the Sun under any circumstances, even with dark sunglasses or through a mirror. However, you can watch a solar eclipse safely by making a device called a pinhole camera. This consists of a piece of cardboard with a pinhole in it. The Sun shines through the hole in the cardboard onto a piece of white paper, where its image appears upside down. When the Sun is completely covered during a solar eclipse, you can see the world turn dark around you, but don't try to look at the Sun.

24

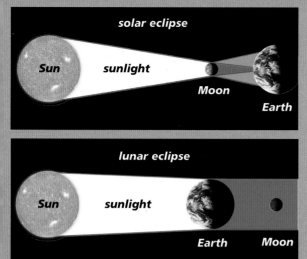

solar eclipse

Sun — sunlight — Moon — Earth

lunar eclipse

Sun — sunlight — Earth — Moon

Shadow play

During a solar eclipse (top), the Moon moves in front of the Sun, blocking its view from Earth. The shadow cast by the Moon races across Earth at hundreds of miles per hour, so the eclipse is over within a couple of minutes. A total eclipse can only be seen by those within the Moon's shadow (dark purple area), while those just outside the shadow will see a partial eclipse. A lunar eclipse (bottom), when Earth passes between the Sun and the Moon, lasts a lot longer since Earth's shadow is so much larger.

When Earth casts its shadow on the Moon, a lunar eclipse occurs. These happen about once a year, and anyone with a view of the Moon can see them. Lunar eclipses are safe to watch.

The Moon doesn't disappear during a lunar eclipse, it just turns dark red or bronze. This is because Earth's shadow does not have a sharp edge—some hazy sunlight is deflected through our atmosphere. The darkest and reddest lunar eclipses happen after volcanoes have flung large amounts of dust and ash into the atmosphere.

Another type of eclipse is an annular eclipse. This is like a total solar eclipse, but the Moon is too small to block the whole Sun and leaves a ring of light visible. Annular eclipses happen because the Moon's orbit is not a perfect circle—when the Moon is furthest away from Earth it appears smaller in the sky.

RIGHT: During an annular eclipse only the center of the Sun is blocked by the Moon.

A Day on the Moon

A full day on the Moon, from one sunrise to the next, lasts about 29 Earth days, on average. Standing on the side of the Moon nearest Earth, you can see your home planet hanging in the sky. It is almost four times the size of a full moon from Earth, and it never moves across the Moon's sky. Using binoculars, you can tell that Earth **rotates** once every 24 hours, and you track continents as they go from day to night and back again. As you watch, the Sun rises slowly in the east. It takes nearly 14 Earth days to track across the Moon's sky before setting in the west. Because there is no **atmosphere** to shield the Moon from the Sun's rays, the surface can reach 230°F (110°C) during the day—hotter than boiling water. Fortunately your spacesuit keeps you cool in the daytime and warm at night, when the temperature can fall as low as –292°F (–180°C).

ABOVE: *With no atmosphere to cloud the view, you can clearly see the daylit half of Earth as it sits above the Moon's horizon.*

toolkit and bags for soil samples

antenna

television camera

BELOW: Apollo 16 *astronaut John Young explores the Moon with the help of the battery-powered Lunar Roving Vehicle. This jeeplike vehicle could travel up to 16 miles (26 kilometers) from the landing site and reached a top speed of 11 miles (18 kilometers) per hour.*

Throughout the long day, your quake-detecting **seismometers** are operating. They show that **moonquakes** reach a peak roughly every 14 Earth days. This puzzles you for a while, but then you figure it out—moonquakes are most violent when the Moon is closest to and furthest away from Earth. This is when the **tidal forces** produced by Earth's **gravity** reach their peak.

Night falls quickly on the Moon because there is no atmosphere to create twilight. Sunlight reflected from Earth prevents the lunar night from becoming pitch black. However, the Earth's glare is not too bright at the moment because it is only half lit during the lunar sunset. Looking in the opposite direction from Earth you can see millions of stars in the sky—many more than are visible from beneath Earth's atmosphere.

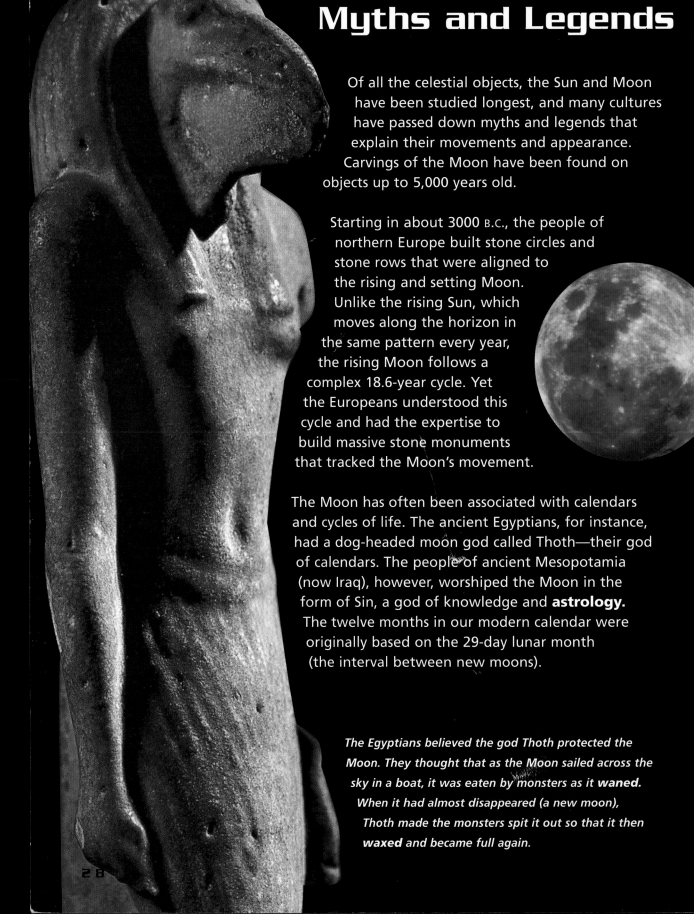

Myths and Legends

Of all the celestial objects, the Sun and Moon have been studied longest, and many cultures have passed down myths and legends that explain their movements and appearance. Carvings of the Moon have been found on objects up to 5,000 years old.

Starting in about 3000 B.C., the people of northern Europe built stone circles and stone rows that were aligned to the rising and setting Moon. Unlike the rising Sun, which moves along the horizon in the same pattern every year, the rising Moon follows a complex 18.6-year cycle. Yet the Europeans understood this cycle and had the expertise to build massive stone monuments that tracked the Moon's movement.

The Moon has often been associated with calendars and cycles of life. The ancient Egyptians, for instance, had a dog-headed moon god called Thoth—their god of calendars. The people of ancient Mesopotamia (now Iraq), however, worshiped the Moon in the form of Sin, a god of knowledge and **astrology.** The twelve months in our modern calendar were originally based on the 29-day lunar month (the interval between new moons).

*The Egyptians believed the god Thoth protected the Moon. They thought that as the Moon sailed across the sky in a boat, it was eaten by monsters as it **waned.** When it had almost disappeared (a new moon), Thoth made the monsters spit it out so that it then **waxed** and became full again.*

28

Eclipse stories

*Many different stories were told to explain solar **eclipses** before astronomers realized they were caused by the Moon. The Chinese thought that the eclipse was caused by an enormous dragon swallowing the Sun (left), and they made as much noise as possible to scare the dragon away. The Mayans of Central America had enough astronomical knowledge to predict eclipses, although not their precise locations, and the Aztecs of Mexico offered human sacrifices in order to encourage the return of the Sun.*

Some people worshiped the Moon as a goddess. The Chinese believed they saw the figure of a woman in the Moon, or sometimes a hare (her sacred animal). The ancient Greeks and Romans had three lunar goddesses to represent the Moon's changing phases. Artemis (or Diana) was the new moon, Selene was the full moon, and Hecate was the dark half of the Moon.

*The Greek moon goddess Selene was often shown wearing a cloak of stars and a **crescent** moon on her head, as in this statue.*

Although these ancient beliefs have been replaced by modern religions, the Moon is still important in folklore and superstition. Astrologers give the Moon the same attributes as ancient lunar gods, and everyone has looked for the face of the "Man in the Moon." Earthshine is sometimes called the "old Moon in the new Moon's arms," and the full Moon is associated with werewolves and other mythical creatures of the night.

LEFT: *The myth that wolves howl at the moon led to the legend of the werewolf—a person who turns into a wolf during a full moon.*

Discoveries from Earth

Because the Moon is so close to Earth, astronomers began to understand it long before they knew much about the rest of the solar system. Early astronomers wrongly thought that everything in the universe **orbited** Earth, but in the Moon's case they were right. By the sixth century B.C. the Greeks understood the Moon enough to predict **eclipses.** In the second century B.C. the Greek astronomer Hipparchus discovered that **phases** were caused by the Moon's movement relative to the Sun. This enabled him to estimate the distance of the Sun and Moon from Earth.

ABOVE: *This fanciful image of the Moon is from the French film Voyage dans la Lune (Trip to the Moon), made in 1902.*

People could see vague patterns on the lunar surface with the naked eye, but the first person to sketch a map of the Moon as it appears through a telescope was probably the English astronomer Thomas Harriot (c.1560–1621) in 1609. Harriot did not publish his observations, and the credit for discovering mountains on the Moon went to the Italian astronomer Galileo Galilei (1564–1642) only a few months later.

Johannes Hevelius (1611–1687)

German astronomer Johannes Hevelius was a wealthy brewing merchant who devoted all his spare time to observing the Moon, sketching its surface, and developing theories about it. He was the first to realize that maria were low, flat plains and that **terrae** *were highlands. He even calculated the heights of some lunar mountains. His observations, including the first accurate lunar maps, were edited and published by his widow in 1690.*

30

As telescopes improved, more and more detail could be seen on the Moon's surface. The **maria** were clearly not seas of water but flat rocky plains, and the highlands were covered in **impact craters.** The first detailed maps of the Moon were compiled in the late 17th century, and as time went by, astronomers gave names to more of the features they saw on its surface.

It soon became clear that the Moon was a dead world, although astronomers saw strange orange glows from time to time that looked like fog or mist. Called transient lunar phenomena (TLPs), these mysterious sightings were often seen around large craters, leading people to think that the craters might be the tops of volcanoes. However, astronomers now think TLPs are just pockets of gas that occasionally burst out from unstable ground. The orange glow is sunlight hitting dust blown up by the gas.

Moon stories

Many people have written stories about journeys to the Moon. As early as the 1600s, English scientist John Wilkins (1614–1672) was fascinated by this idea, but the most famous books on the subject came much later. In From the Earth to the Moon *(1873) by French author Jules Verne (1828–1905), the heroes were fired into space from a huge cannon, while English author H.G. Wells (1866–1946) invented an anti-**gravity** spaceship for his book* The First Men in the Moon *(1901). This book featured a race of underground Moon-people called Selenites, one of whom is shown here (left) in a 1964 film version of Wells's book.*

31

Race for the Moon

When the U.S. and the Soviet Union sent the first **space probes** and **astronauts** into space in the 1950s and 1960s, the Moon was an obvious target. The two nations were locked in the Cold War—a struggle for worldwide political influence. Both sides thought they might gain some kind of advantage by taking the lead in the Space Race.

ABOVE: *The Russian space probe* Luna 2 *was the first probe to reach the Moon's surface. It crash-landed on the Moon in 1959.*

The first space probes to the Moon were sent by the Soviets in 1959. *Luna 1* missed the Moon by 3,000 miles (5,000 kilometers), but *Luna 2* hit it, and *Luna 3* swung around behind the Moon, returning the first pictures of the far side on October 4, 1959. Then the Soviet Union hit a run of bad luck—*Lunas 4* to *8* all failed to make soft landings on the Moon. This gave NASA a chance to catch up.

Almost as soon as the U.S. had launched its first astronaut in May 1961, President John F. Kennedy (1917–1963) set the goal of putting an American on the Moon by the end of the decade. Rocket technology in the U.S. was then trailing far behind that of the Soviets, so NASA launched a major space program to develop rockets and spacecraft that were capable of reaching the Moon.

Sergei Pavlovich Korolev (1907–1966)

The early Soviet lead in the Space Race was primarily due to the engineering genius of Sergei Korolev. In the 1930s many of Russia's most intelligent men and women—including Korolev—were persecuted by the communist leader Josef Stalin. Korolev was exiled to a work camp in Siberia, but because of his expertise he was called back to design rockets for the army. His main interest, however, was space exploration. After his success in designing long-range missiles, he adapted his rockets to make spacecraft. His rockets were used to launch the very first satellite into space.

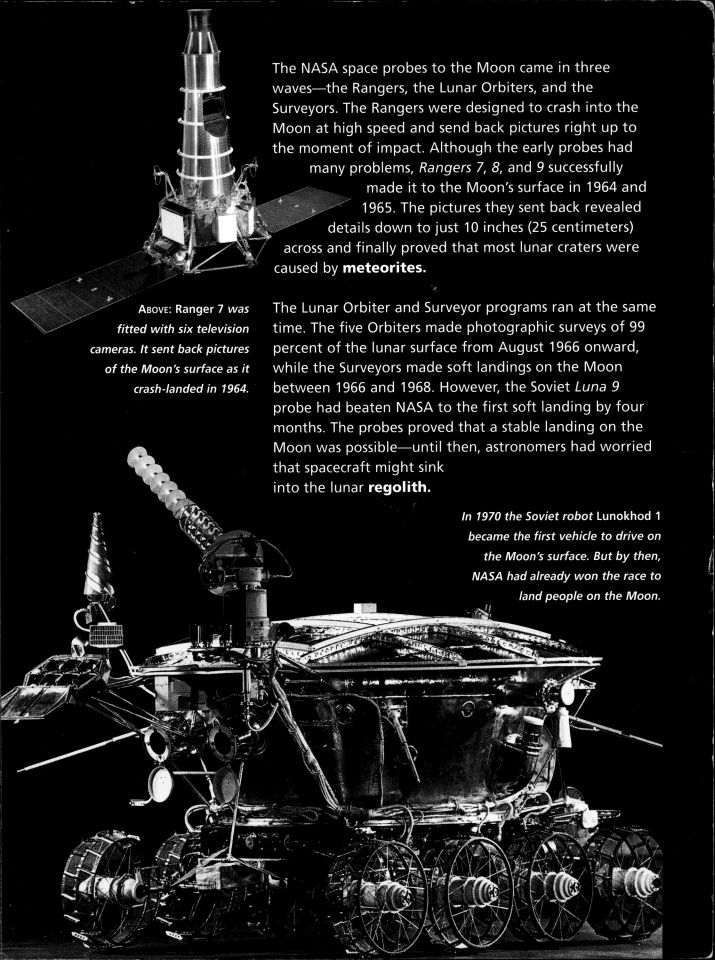

The NASA space probes to the Moon came in three waves—the Rangers, the Lunar Orbiters, and the Surveyors. The Rangers were designed to crash into the Moon at high speed and send back pictures right up to the moment of impact. Although the early probes had many problems, *Rangers 7*, *8*, and *9* successfully made it to the Moon's surface in 1964 and 1965. The pictures they sent back revealed details down to just 10 inches (25 centimeters) across and finally proved that most lunar craters were caused by **meteorites.**

ABOVE: **Ranger 7** *was fitted with six television cameras. It sent back pictures of the Moon's surface as it crash-landed in 1964.*

The Lunar Orbiter and Surveyor programs ran at the same time. The five Orbiters made photographic surveys of 99 percent of the lunar surface from August 1966 onward, while the Surveyors made soft landings on the Moon between 1966 and 1968. However, the Soviet *Luna 9* probe had beaten NASA to the first soft landing by four months. The probes proved that a stable landing on the Moon was possible—until then, astronomers had worried that spacecraft might sink into the lunar **regolith.**

In 1970 the Soviet robot **Lunokhod 1** *became the first vehicle to drive on the Moon's surface. But by then, NASA had already won the race to land people on the Moon.*

Apollo and After

During the 1960s, NASA put huge amounts of time and money into preparing its crewed lunar **missions,** called the Apollo program. **Astronauts** trained in **orbit** aboard the one-man *Mercury* and two-man *Gemini* spacecraft, while engineers on the ground designed a three-part spacecraft to carry the astronauts to the Moon, and built huge *Saturn V* rockets 363 feet (111 meters) high to launch these spacecraft.

ABOVE: *During each mission, the Apollo spacecraft split into a command module (above), which stayed in orbit around the Moon, and a lunar module, which landed on the surface.*

The triumph of the Apollo program finally came on July 20, 1969, when the spindly *Apollo 11* Lunar Module (named Eagle) landed on the Moon, and astronauts Neil Armstrong and Edwin "Buzz" Aldrin stepped out onto the surface for the first time.

Armstrong and Aldrin stayed for just a few hours, but later *Apollo* missions lasted much longer. Astronauts collected large amounts of moon rocks for study on Earth, set up **seismometers** to detect **moonquakes,** and even drove a special Lunar Roving Vehicle on the Moon.

BELOW: *Astronaut James Irwin salutes during the* Apollo 15 *mission of 1971.*

The Apollo program ended with *Apollo 17* in 1972. Meanwhile, the Soviets abandoned their plans for a manned lunar landing, although they sent several Luna **space probes** to collect rock samples and return them to Earth. By 1976 Moon missions had stopped. Interest was reignited when the *Galileo* probe flew past the Moon in 1990 and 1992. This was followed by two more missions in the late 1990s.

34

Neil Armstrong (1930–)

In July 1969 Neil Armstrong became the first person to set foot on the Moon, with the famous words "That's one small step for [a] man, one giant leap for mankind." He had been a pilot in the U.S. Navy before joining NASA and being selected as an astronaut in 1962. Although Armstrong left NASA in 1971, he was recalled in 1986 to run the investigation into the Challenger *space shuttle explosion.*

Clementine was a U.S. Department of Defense probe designed to test "Star Wars" technology, but also sent to study the Moon. It was equipped with sophisticated instruments to identify lunar **minerals** and map the Moon's surface. These instruments revealed the Moon in a new light—for the first time, astronomers could map the location of different rock types on the Moon and see the Moon's **poles** in detail.

Clementine was followed by *Lunar Prospector,* which added yet more detail to our knowledge of the Moon and found tantalizing evidence that ice may exist there, hidden in shadow at the bottom of large craters.

BELOW: *Astronaut Eugene Cernan drives the Lunar Roving Vehicle during the* Apollo 17 *mission of 1972. He was the last person to stand on the Moon's surface.*

35

Could Humans Live There?

People are likely to return to the Moon in the near future, and perhaps next time they will be going to stay. Because the Moon is on our cosmic doorstep, it would be relatively simple to establish an airtight base there and provide it with supplies, crews, and equipment. Although scientists have not yet found definite proof of ice on the Moon, many are convinced that it is there. Ice could be a valuable resource, providing not just water and oxygen, but also hydrogen, which can be used as fuel.

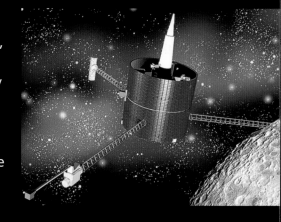

Although the Moon's **gravity** is low, it is strong enough to keep **astronauts'** bodies working efficiently and so prevent the kind of health problems that long periods of weightlessness can cause. The main danger would be **radiation** from the Sun, but shields could be placed around the Moon base, or the entire base could be built underground for protection.

A Moon colony could be used as a base for exploring the solar system, and telescopes on the far side would provide fine views of the depths of space. Also, **satellites** have detected rare minerals on the Moon that could be mined.

ABOVE: *The Lunar Prospector probe, shown in this artwork, crashed into the Moon to test for water. Lunar water would make it easier for us to live there.*

BELOW: *This artist's impression, showing a cut-away interior of an inflatable moonbase, reveals (from bottom up) astronauts' living quarters, two floors for growing food, a laboratory, and a gym for keeping fit in the weak gravity of the Moon.*

Glossary

asteroid large chunk of rock left over from when the planets formed

asteroid belt ring of asteroids that orbit the Sun between the orbits of Mars and Jupiter

astrology ancient tradition in which the positions of the planets, moons, and stars are thought to influence people and events or reveal the future

astronaut person trained to go into space

atmosphere layer of gas trapped by gravity around the surface of a planet or moon

axis imaginary line through the middle of a planet or moon that it spins around

basalt type of rock formed from lava

basin very large impact crater

breccia boulder formed by compression of rock dust during a meteorite impact

comet large chunk of ice left over from when the planets formed

core center of a planet or moon

crescent curved shape like one segment of an orange

crust solid outer surface of a planet or moon

debris fragments of rock, dust, ice, or other materials

dense having a lot of weight squeezed into a small space

diameter width of an object measured by drawing a straight line through its center

eclipse effect caused by a planet or moon moving in front of the Sun and casting a shadow on another object

ejecta blanket material thrown out during the formation of an impact crater

element chemical that cannot be split into other chemicals

ellipse stretched circle, or oval

equator imaginary line around the center of a planet or moon midway between the poles

gravity force that pulls objects together. The heavier or closer an object is, the stronger its gravity, or pull.

impact crater crater made when an object from space crashes into a planet or moon

lander spacecraft that lands on a moon or planet

late heavy bombardment period in the early solar system when planets and moons were bombarded by space debris

lava molten rock on a planet's surface

magnetic field region around a planet, moon, or star where a compass can detect the north pole

mantle part of a planet or moon located between the core and the crust

maria (singular mare) smooth, dark plains created by huge floods of lava that swept across the surface of the Moon; also called seas

meteor small piece of space rock that burns up in a planet's atmosphere

meteorite space rock that lands on the surface of a planet or moon

micrometeorite tiny meteorite less than a millimeter in diameter

mineral type of solid chemical found in rock

mission expedition to visit a specific target in space, such as a planet, moon, or asteroid

moonquake like an earthquake, only it takes place on the Moon

neap tide lesser high tide that occurs during the first and third quarters of the Moon

orbit path an object takes around a larger object; or, to take such a path

phase area of a planet or moon that is lit by the Sun

pole point on the surface of a planet that coincides with the top or bottom end of its axis

radiation energy released in rays from a source. Heat and light are types of radiation.

regolith top layer of fragmented rocky soil on the Moon formed from meteorite impacts

rotate to turn around

satellite object that orbits a planet

seismometer instrument used to detect shockwaves moving through the ground on a moon or planet

shockwave powerful pulse of energy that spreads out from an explosion, collision, or other source

space probe robotic vehicle sent from Earth to study the solar system

spring tide particularly high tide that occurs at the new and full moons

terminator line that divides night from day on the Moon

terrae crater-covered highlands between the lunar maria

terrestrial like Earth

tidal force pull exerted on the surface of a planet or moon by the gravity of another moon or planet nearby, or by the Sun

waning lunar phase in which the sunlit part of the Moon is getting smaller

waxing lunar phase in which the sunlit part of the Moon is getting larger

More Books to Read

Bourgeois, Paulette. *The Moon.* Niagara Falls, New York: Kids Can Press, 1999.
Cole, Michael D. *First Moon Landing.* Berkeley Heights, N.J.: Enslow Publishers Inc., 1995.
Couper, Heather, and Henbest, Nigel. *The DK Space Encyclopedia*. New York: Dorling Kindersley, 1999.
Kerrod, Robin. *The Moon.* Minneapolis, Minn.: Lerner Publications Company, 2000.
Seymour, Simon. *The Solar System.* New York: William Morris, 1992.

Index